ADVENT IS FOR CHILDREN

Stories, Activities, Prayers

Julie Kelemen

Liguori
ONE LIGUORI DRIVE
LIGUORI MO 63057-9999

Dedication

To Saints
Frances Xavier Cabrini
and Anthony of Padua
and the friends and relatives
who introduced them to me.

Imprimi Potest:
Stephen T. Palmer, C.SS.R.
Provincial, St. Louis Province
The Redemptorists

Imprimatur:
Monsignor Maurice F. Byrne
Vice Chancellor, Archdiocese of St. Louis

ISBN 978-0-89243-292-9
Library of Congress Catalog Card Number: 88-81402

Cover design: Larry Nolte, Interior artwork: Larry Nolte

Liguori Publications, a nonprofit corporation, is an apostolate of the Redemptorists. To learn more about the Redemptorists, visit Redemptorists.com.

To order, call 800-325-9521 or visit www.liguori.org

Table of Contents

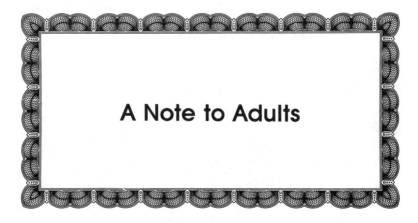

A Note to Adults

Advent is often compared to Lent because these are the liturgical seasons that prepare Christians for the two most celebrated days of the Christian calendar — Christmas and Easter. In fact, Advent and Lent are very different in focus. While Lent is primarily a penitential season, Advent has a more mystical, anticipatory tone than Lent. It is important to resist the temptation simply to make Advent a pre-Christmas Lent.

Children need activities and tangible things to help them understand the intangibles of our faith. Adults are greatly helped by this, too, and so in this way we are all children of God who can learn from a booklet like this. Explaining the significance of Advent to children can be more challenging than explaining Lent but the task is not impossible. You can do it! Children love to hear stories about when the adults in their lives were young. Speak of the things you remember about your childhood Advents. The coming of Christmas is more than a wreath, a baby in a crib, a tree, shepherds, and gifts. It speaks of *preparation, coming,* and *hope*. This booklet suggests many activities to make the coming of Christ come alive for Christians young and old.

Explaining Advent is made more difficult because it lasts four full weeks or less and comes at a time of great activity. While the official liturgical season of Advent cannot be extended, the religious preparation time for Christmas can easily be extended by several weeks. As soon as stores put up decorations and TV commercials start advertising Christmas gifts, you can begin to use this booklet. It is good to prepare *now* and *always* for the coming of God's kingdom, regardless of whether Christmas is right around the corner or ten weeks away.

1. Turning on the Light

*Jesus Is a Symbol of Light
for the World*

"Let Jerry put the candles on the cake," Mom said, shooing away the other kids from the kitchen counter.

"But I want to do it this time, Mom. I want to light the candles. I'm big enough," said Beth, Jerry's little sister.

"When it's time for you to put nine candles on your own birthday cake, then you can do it," said Dad. "This time you can watch very closely and see how it's done, then you'll know how to do it when you're older."

Beth ran to the table and Jerry waited with the matches as Mom and Dad brought the cake and ice cream to the table. Jerry then poked the candles into the cake and carefully lit the match. The match hissed into a big orange flame and then quickly died down to just a tiny fire. Beth leaned over the table and watched very closely. Jerry lit one of the candles and then blew out the match. Just as Mom and Dad had always done, Jerry picked up the one lit candle. He lit all the other candles with just that one candle.

It seemed kind of odd to Beth that one tiny flame could light so many other candles. Jerry could have easily lit twenty more candles with just the one. Beth wondered why the first candle could light so many others yet still stay burning itself. She figured she would understand it better when she grew up. Beth stopped thinking about the candles and began to sing "Happy Birthday" with the rest of her family.

Jesus Is Light for the World

A light can do many things. Some lights help us see when it is dark. Others give us a special message, like a green traffic light that says it's okay to "go." In comics or cartoons a light bulb sometimes appears over a person's head to show that someone has a bright new idea. People talk about being *enlightened* or they say, "Now I see the light."

Light is very special to Jesus. In fact, Jesus is often called the *Light of the World*. When Jesus is called the Light of the World it doesn't mean that he glowed in the dark or anything like that.

Light of the World means that Jesus was *like* a light or a lit candle. In the story about the birthday cake, Jerry was able to light many candles from just one flame. When we call Jesus the Light of the World that means that Christ's love works like a candle flame. From one flame many other candles can be lit. Each new light can light many others. Jesus loves you and shares his light and his love with you and with all other Christians. If you pass that light on to others, they can pass it on to even more people, and so on — just like lighting candles on a cake. Jesus is like the first candle who gives out light to all the rest.

When people call Jesus the Light of the World they also mean that he was the bright light that helped people see the right way to live. In a world that was filled with confusion and sadness, Jesus came like a shining light to bring help and hope to all people. We can receive that light and guidance from Jesus and pass it along to others, too.

The Christmas lights that people put up during Advent can remind us that *people* spread Jesus' love and light here on earth. Jesus gives his love and light to us and we can pass it on to others in little ways. We can be the light that brightens an older person's day by shoveling their snow or doing their shopping. We can bring the light of Christ to a younger brother or sister by helping them with their homework or reading them a story from the Bible.

A Symbol of Light for Advent

Take a look at the pictures below and see if you can say, in a few words, what each one stands for.

A symbol is something that stands for something else. In the pictures above, the Cross is a symbol for Jesus; the road sign is a symbol for the words, "Caution! Deer cross here!"; and the finger sign means "okay."

The most famous symbol of Advent is the Advent wreath. This wreath is often made from evergreen branches and decorated with four candles. The candles remind us that Jesus, the Light of the World, is coming. For every week of Advent, we light another candle until all the candles are lit on the Sunday before Christmas.

Something to Do —
Making Your Own Advent Wreath

Have you ever noticed that homemade cookies often taste better than the ones you buy at the store? Well, the same thing is true for Advent wreaths, too (except you're not supposed to eat an Advent wreath). Although ready-made wreaths can be bought, it can be more fun to make your own. Make sure your wreath is made before the First Sunday of Advent if you want to get the best use out of it, but if it's a little late, that's okay.

Supplies:

- 6 to 8 evergreen boughs, all between 6″ and 12″ long
- A wire coat hanger
- Lots of green twist ties (Twist ties are the little paper or plastic-covered wires that seal trash bags.)

- Three purple candles
- One pink or rose-colored candle
- Small candle holders or four lumps of clay that can be formed into low candle holders
- A red ribbon

Directions:

1. Shape the coat hanger into a circle. Bend the hook toward the inside of the circle or have an adult clip it off for you.
2. Fasten the evergreens to the coat hanger with the twist ties until you have a nice green wreath.
3. Attach the red bow to the wreath.
4. Put the candles into their holders and place the candles in the wreath.

Advent Wreath Ceremonies:

There is no official way that the Advent wreath *must* be used. Your class or family can decide on a way to use the wreath that fits your needs. At home, some people place their wreath in the middle of the dinner table, on top of the TV, or on a special table of its own. In a classroom, the wreath can be placed on a windowsill or on its own special table. Pick a convenient time when you will light the wreath and spend a few moments in prayer. For families, before the evening meal is often a good time. The beginning of class is a good time for lighting an Advent wreath in school.

Each time the wreath is lighted select one person to light the candle, one to read a short passage from the Bible, and one to say a prayer. The wreath can be lighted once a week or every day. Light one purple candle for the first week and two purple candles the second week. For the third week, light the pink candle and two purple candles. Light all the candles during the fourth week of Advent. By increasing the number of candles the wreath reminds us that the coming of Christ the Light is drawing closer.

Prayer

Dear Jesus, now I know what you mean about light — *your* light is good and it helps me see every day. Thank you for the beautiful Christmas lights in stores and homes. Thank you also for the good people who bring light to me. Help me to remember that your light is in me, too, and that I can help turn on your light for others. Amen.

2. On the Lookout for Jesus

Advent Is a Time to Watch and Be Alert

The word *advent* goes all the way back to those people who spoke Latin in ancient Rome. Back then the word was *advenire* and it simply meant "to come toward." *Venire* means "to come" and *ad* means "to" or "toward." Using the word in a slightly different way, a Latin speaker could tell a dog to "Come here!" by saying, *"Huc veni!"*

Today, when anyone uses the word advent they use it to talk about something that is coming. Of course advent doesn't mean just any old thing is coming (like a late school bus). Advent talks about something really important that is coming. Sometimes you'll hear grown-ups talking about things like "the advent of technology" or "the advent of the space age."

In the Church, we put a capital "A" at the beginning of the word Advent. When you see that, you can be sure that someone is talking about the four-week season that comes before Christmas.

Something to Do —
Advent Words

The letters of all the words described below can be made from the letters in the word *Advent*. Honest! Each of the words has a Bible verse after the clue to help you find the word. Even if you can guess the answer, locate and read the passage in the Bible.

ADVENT

1. One small insect is an __ __ __ (Proverbs 6:6).

2. Some of the apostles caught fish with a __ __ __ (John 21:6).

3. The number of Commandments is __ __ __ (Exodus 20:2-17).

4. A huge container that wine or grain is stored in is a __ __ __ (Haggai 2:16).

5. The Israelites sometimes traveled in a __ __ __ (Numbers 32:17).

6. A cobra lives in a __ __ __ (Isaiah 11:8).

7. A nickname for Jesus' friend Nathaniel could be __ __ __ (John 1:45).

8. To release anger is to __ __ __ __ (Hosea 11:9).

9. Christ's reign will not have an __ __ __ (Luke 1:33).

10. Father, Son, __ __ __ Holy Spirit (Matthew 28:19).

Advent Reminds Us of Three Comings

Advent lasts for about four weeks. It begins four Sundays before Christmas and ends on Christmas Day. It is a time to help us get ready for the coming of Christ at Christmas, but it is also much more than that.

If you listen closely to what the priest and lector read from the Bible at Mass during Advent you may be a little surprised. Not many of the stories have much to do with Jesus when he was a baby. Part of the reason for that is that we simply don't know very much about Jesus when he was growing up.

Another reason the readings don't say much about Baby Jesus is because Advent isn't just about the coming of a baby. It is also a time when we are reminded about how Jesus comes to us each day. When we pray, when we go to church, when we see the beauty of all the things God created, when we do good things for other people, and when other people help us, we see Christ coming into our lives and our world. Advent also reminds us that this world will not last forever. When it ends, Christ will come a final time to bring people home with him. Advent reminds us of Christ coming in three ways:

1. Christ came to earth and was born in Bethlehem.

2. Christ comes to us today as we live our lives as good Christians.

3. Christ will come again at the end of time.

Advent Is a Time to Prepare

Every day when you wake up, it's time to prepare for a new day. On school days that means doing things like waking up early, putting on school clothes, getting books or lunch ready, and eating breakfast. Perhaps it's your responsibility to feed the cat or make your bed, too. Then you put on a coat if it's cold out, or maybe you take an umbrella if it's raining. Preparing for school can mean running to the bus stop or helping your mom or dad scrape ice off the windshield. There sure is a lot to do just to get ready for one day! It's amazing that we even make it out the door with all those things to do! And that's just a regular, ordinary day!

Something to Do — Make an Advent Calendar

One way to prepare for the coming of Christ is to make and use an Advent calendar. Ready-made Advent calendars can be bought at the store, but it's more fun to make your own. Here's one you can make for your family to use this year. You may want to ask an adult for help with this project.

Supplies:

- Two 8½ x 11 inch sheets of construction paper, one white and one dark blue. If you don't have blue construction paper, use any heavy paper and color it dark blue to show it is night.
- Colored pencils, markers, crayons, or chalk
- Ruler
- Scissors
- Paste
- Transparent tape
- Single-edge razor blade or X-ACTO knife

Directions:

1. In the top right-hand corner on the blue paper, draw a yellow or white star or paste on a cut-out star — like the Magi followed to find Jesus. Make the star a big one that will be easy for people to see when they look at the picture. Add rays of light coming from the star. To the left of the star, print in large letters: COME, LORD JESUS.

2. On the other sheet of paper, draw or paste on a picture of the nativity scene (Mary, Joseph, Baby Jesus in the manger, and so forth). Make the picture a big one so that it covers most of the paper.

3. On the back side of the paper with the star on it, draw six rows of boxes with five boxes in each row. If you make each box 1¼ inch long and 1 inch wide, they should all fit nicely. These boxes become the doors of your Advent calendar.

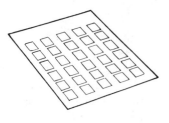

4. Cut three sides of each door, leaving one side uncut so it is still attached to the big piece of paper on that side. Ask an adult to help you with the razor blade or knife.

5. Carefully paste the edges of the two pieces of paper together, one on top of the other. Paste the picture of the star on top of the picture of the nativity scene. In this way, when you open the doors you will see parts of the nativity scene. (If you prefer, you could use tape instead of paste.)

6. Tape all the doors shut with tiny bits of tape.

7. Write a small number on each door (from one to thirty). You can number the doors in order or mix up the numbers just as long as you use the numbers one to thirty.

Using Your Advent Calendar:

Think of how you and your family get ready for an important event like Christmas Day. How do you help get the house ready? How do you get yourself ready? What plans must be made?

Make a list of all the things that you or anyone else in your home does during Advent to prepare for Christmas. When you run out of ideas, ask other people in your family what they do to prepare for Christmas. If they think of any things that you haven't thought of, write those things on your list, too. Now compare your list to the list in this book. Are you surprised at how many things people have to do to get ready for Christmas?

For each day of Advent, select one thing to do. It can be something from your personal list or from the list in the book. When you prepare for the coming of Christ by completing that action, you can open a door on your Advent calendar.

Since there will be less than thirty days in Advent you can start a few days before the official beginning of Advent or you can open the extra doors on days when you have been extra good! On Christmas Eve you should open the final doors.

A List of Advent Practices:

1. Help decorate the Christmas tree.
2. Read about Jesus in the Bible for ten minutes.
3. Read a Christmas story.
4. Pray for a relative or friend who is ill and for the person's family. Ask Christ to bring them the joy and peace of Christmas.
5. Help send Christmas cards.
6. Say "I'm sorry" to someone you've hurt.
7. Prepare for the next day of school by finishing your homework before you watch TV.
8. Prepare for tomorrow by going to bed on time so you get plenty of rest.
9. Prepare to welcome guests at your home by cleaning up your room.
10. Prepare your heart for the coming of Christ. Celebrate the sacrament of Reconciliation by going to confession.

For the rest of the days of Advent, prepare for the coming of Christ by doing one of the things on your personal list or one of the other activities suggested in this book.

Prayer

Dear Jesus, when I look at the calendar and see how long it is until Christmas, I just can't wait! I want school to be finished but it's only ten o'clock in the morning. Some days I want so much to see and touch you when I talk with you. I feel like I can't wait until Christmas when you will come in a special way to my heart. I know Christmas always comes, and the school day does end, and I know, in my heart, that waiting is something everyone must do. As the days on the Advent calendar go by, help me remember the other people who wait for you to come to their lives — the sick, the lonely, the elderly, the poor. Show me how I can best use this waiting time to prepare for your birth and help others prepare for your coming to our world. Amen.

3. A Journey in a Time Machine

The Hebrew People Wait for the Messiah

Did you know that the first Advent lasted for hundreds of years? That's because the Hebrew people (also called the Israelites or the Jews or the Chosen People) waited centuries for Jesus the Messiah to be born.

Can you imagine waiting hundreds of years for Christmas to come? That's what the people we read about in the Hebrew Scriptures (also called the Old Testament) did. People like Moses, Abraham, Ruth, Isaac, and Job waited all their lives and never saw the birth of the Savior. While these people waited for years and years they tried always to be on guard. They watched, waited, and prepared for the Messiah.

Some of the most important people who hoped for the birth of the Messiah were the *prophets*. They had names like Daniel, Isaiah, Jeremiah, and Ezekiel. If you pick up a Bible you'll see that there are books named after these special men.

The prophets were those men who spoke to the people about the coming of the Messiah. Filled with the Spirit of God they told the people how to get ready for the Savior's arrival. While they did not know the exact date of Jesus' arrival, they knew that the people should honor God and love their neighbor in order to prepare for the coming of the Messiah.

Sometimes, when life was very hard, the prophets told the people they didn't need to be afraid because God loved them and would be with them during their struggles. At other times the prophets got mad at the people and told them to stop their evil ways. They warned that if they didn't change their ways, God would be very unhappy with them.

Isaiah, one of the most important prophets, was a very smart man who gave advice to the rulers of the day. He also gave the people hope for a better future by telling them about the Messiah.

Many people felt that the prophet Jeremiah was a pretty scary guy. They did not like the fact that he was always hollering at them. What did he holler about? Well, he knew that the Hebrew people living in Jerusalem didn't appreciate God's special gifts to them. They were all sitting around saying to themselves, "Hey, we're the Chosen People and we're really great! *We* don't have to worry about anybody taking over our city because God says we're special and Jerusalem is ours." Through the words of Jeremiah, God was trying to tell the people that they were headed for destruction. The people didn't listen to Jeremiah and, sure enough, enemies attacked Jerusalem. They chased the Hebrews out of their city and forced them to move far away to another country to live.

Daniel was another fa-mous prophet. He spent much of his life trying to get people who didn't even believe in God to start be-lieving. The Bible stories about Daniel are some of the most interesting ones around. Not only did Daniel have to deal with non-believers, but also with lions and a dragon! (You can read this story in the Book of Daniel, chapter 14, verses 23 to 42.)

As you can see from reading about some of these prophets, the Hebrew people's life was pretty tough. At various times in history they were slaves. At other times they had no place to call home. They lost wars and suffered defeats, but the prophets and other religious leaders encouraged them to keep hoping for the coming of the Messiah.

We Await
the Final Coming of Christ

We know that Jesus has already come to our world as a human person. He was here on this earth for about 33 years until he was put to death on the Cross. Jesus also comes to touch our lives today when we pray, go to Mass, or see God's goodness around us. Like the Hebrew people, however, we still wait for the coming of Christ. We wait for him to come into our lives and our world.

Christians have now been waiting for nearly 2,000 years. We, too, may die before Christ comes again. In this way, all of life is one long Advent season. The Advent season every year reminds us that we should always be prepared for Christ's final coming.

Something to Do —
In Search of the Final Coming

The Bible has many things to say about the end of the world and Christ's final coming. Some of those things can be found in these Bible passages:

- Matthew 24:37-44
- Matthew 25:31-46
- Mark 13:24-27
- John 14:1-7
- 1 Thessalonians 4:13-18
- Revelation 7:1-17

1. Look up each Bible passage and see what it says. You can make a game out of it, if you like, by seeing if you can find and read the passages in fifteen minutes or less.
2. Once you've read the passages, draw a picture of what you think the final coming will be like. If you like to write more than you like to draw, write a story about this event.

The Ones Who Prepared
the Way for Jesus

"Now it is my greatest pleasure and honor to introduce that man we've all been waiting for, the promised one, the man who will do nothing less than save us from ourselves. Here he is, the one, the only. . . . "

Whom do you think that introduction could be for? A famous singer? The president? A circus act? Such an announcement is certainly saying that we should sit up and take notice of a very special person. But who?

Without announcers life could be very confusing. Just try watching a ball game on TV without the sound of the announcer's voice. Pretty boring, right? If there was a fire in your school you could be in terrible danger if there weren't an alarm to "announce" the sound that would tell everyone to get out of the building. A telephone would be pretty useless if it had no ringer to announce that someone was trying to call.

God knew that announcers would be needed to help people prepare to welcome Jesus.

Shortly before Jesus arrived on earth God sent a few important "announcers" to tell people to prepare for the birth of Christ. The Archangel Gabriel announced to Mary that she would be Jesus' Mother. On the very night that Jesus was born a group of angels announced to the shepherds that Christ had been born in a stable. A special star announced to the Wise Men that the new King had been born. There was also an actual person — someone with skin on — who announced to people that Jesus was coming. He was John the Baptizer.

The Final Messenger Arrives

John the Baptizer was born about the same time as Jesus, so he could hardly announce the birth of Jesus. What he announced was the coming of Jesus as a preacher and healer. John baptized people in the Jordan River and warned folks that they'd better clean up their act before Jesus got there. "Make ready the way of the Lord," he told them.

God did people a big favor by sending John out to be the announcer for Jesus. If it hadn't been for John, people wouldn't have known that the Messiah was among them.

John the Baptizer would probably be called weird today. He lived by himself in the desert, not far from the Dead Sea. John wore clothes made out of camel hair, which is itchy, uncomfortable, and hot for someone who lives in the desert. On top of all that he ate mostly grasshoppers and wild honey! Because he was so odd a lot of people went out to see him and figure out what he was doing. John's (and God's) plan worked — once the people got out to John, he would loudly preach to them, saying that they should let him wash away their sins so that they could be prepared for Jesus. You can read more about John in the Gospels of Matthew 3:1-17; Mark 1:1-11; Luke 1:5-25, 57-80; and John 1:6-12, 15-37.

Why Didn't John Baptize Babies and Children?

The kind of baptizing John did was a bit different from the baptism you probably received as a baby. When John baptized people, he dunked them in the river. He did this as a sign of their willingness to change their evil ways.

Today Catholics are usually baptized as babies so that they can start following Christ's ways from the very beginning of their lives. Baptism is the sign that they are filled with the life of Christ and reborn into the Christian community as children of God.

The cleansing that was part of John's baptism for adults might remind you of what happens during the sacrament of Reconciliation. You confess your sins to the priest, ask the Lord for help, and promise to try to live a better Christian life. Advent is a good time to receive this sacrament. It is an important way to prepare for the coming of Christ at Christmas. It is also a way to let Christ come into your life more fully as you think about how much he loves you and wants to help you as you try to be good and do what is right.

Something to Do —
Your Gift to Baby Jesus

"Dear Jesus,"

At Christmastime, a lot of children write a letter to Santa in which they list all the gifts they hope to get. Here's a new kind of letter, one you'll write to Jesus instead. Imagine that Jesus was going to be born *this* Christmas. (Of course, he was born almost 2,000 years ago, but you can always imagine!) In your letter to Jesus, tell him:

1. about the people in the world who need his help the most;
2. how he could help you, your family, friends, and classmates;
3. how you will help others to know about Christ, the Light of the World;
4. what you will do to prepare for his coming at Christmas.

Writing a letter to Jesus is a bit like praying. You can also write letters that are like prayers to Mary and the saints. You can use this way to pray when you don't feel like using the sitting-still-with-your-eyes-shut type of prayer.

Prayer

Dear Jesus, I'm not a baby anymore, but I'm not an adult yet, either. Sometimes it's hard waiting to grow up. It would be really neat if I could drive *now,* or stay up as late as I want *now,* or see any kind of movies I want to see *now.* We kids get so anxious to grow up that we sometimes end up doing something wrong like wandering away from home without telling anyone, or doing careless things like playing with matches or riding bikes on a really busy street. I'm sorry for the times I got too anxious to grow up and ended up sinning. Help me to love being young because I'll probably be an adult a lot longer than I'll be a kid! Amen.

4. A Girl Becomes Part of Jesus' Life

Mary, the Mother of God

It was evening and most people were in their homes wiping the last bread crumbs from dinner dishes or putting babies to bed. These were the times before electric lights — shortly before Jesus came into the world. If people needed light in the evening they lit candles or oil lamps. The only sound in the narrow, rocky streets was made by some dogs skittering around and growling at each other as they fought over scraps of roast lamb bones. The full moon cast a gentle silver light onto the sides of the homes.

Although the streets were pretty quiet, a young man in his twenties shuffled along. His eyebrows were wrinkled up from worry. He was on his way to nowhere in particular . . . just thinking very deeply. He was to be married soon and the wonderful girl he had asked to be his wife was in big trouble. In fact, she was in danger of losing her life. She wasn't married yet but she was going to have a baby. That wasn't supposed to happen! In those days, if a woman became pregnant before marriage, she was punished in one of the worst ways possible. The law said people had to throw rocks at her until she died.

The man walked on worrying and wondering. He knew he had to make a decision soon. He wanted to cry. His plans for a wonderful life, his dreams of being a dad — everything he had hoped for seemed to be broken into a million pieces that no glue could ever put together again. He stroked his beard and wondered what had gone wrong.

Have you ever felt angry, sad, afraid, hurt, and puzzled all at the same time? That's how this young man felt.

He asked God how such a terrible thing could happen. He wondered how God could shape the beautiful heavens and the shining moon and yet not change this terrible situation. Finally, the man decided on what he would do. He would call off the marriage, but he would do it quietly so that the pregnant girl wouldn't be killed. It was the right thing to do.

When he arrived home he went to bed immediately. Tired from so much worrying, he was soon asleep. During the night he had a dream. The dream was so vivid that he would remember it and tell stories about it for the rest of his life. In the dream a great burst of warm light shone. From within the light a voice told him not to be afraid, but to go ahead and marry the girl. God would make things right and protect them in a special way.

The man was Joseph, the pregnant girl was Mary, and the baby she would have was Jesus. If you'd like to read the whole story about Joseph's worry and how the angel visited him, read Matthew 1:18-25. This is one of the few times that Joseph, the foster-father of Jesus, is mentioned in the Bible.

Mary Is More Than a Statue

Every year, shortly before Christmas, most churches set up something called a "creche" (pronounced "kresh"). The creche is made up of statues of Mary, Joseph, the three Magi, shepherds, farm animals, and the manger where they placed the newborn infant Jesus. Now *everyone* knows that those statues aren't the real people. They are just plastic or plaster images that help us remember the birth of Jesus. The problem is that since those people are not here on earth with us, many people (grown-ups included) find it hard to think of

Mary or the others as having been *real* people. We know the statue of Mary isn't really Mary, but do we also know that Mary wasn't really a statue? Try to understand that Mary was a real person who worked, played, prayed, and prepared for adult life just as you do. It might be easier for you to think of Mary as a real person if you remember that she probably was no more than ten years older than you when she gave birth to Jesus. It is also rather likely that Joseph wasn't that much older than Mary. People married at a younger age back then.

The story at the beginning of this chapter may have surprised you a lot. If it did, don't be upset. Just try to remember that Mary and Joseph were real people — maybe like your parents in some ways!

Something to Do — A Bible Treasure Hunt

You'll need a Bible for this treasure hunt if you hope to find the places where Mary is mentioned in the Bible. If you don't know how to find Bible verses, ask someone to show you. It's as easy as looking up something in the TV guide or the dictionary once you know how.

Look up the following verses. On the line beside the Bible verse write down how Mary is mentioned in the story you found. The first one has been done for you. If you want to race against yourself, see how many you can find in 15 minutes. Two or more people or a whole class can compete to see who is the fastest.

1. Matthew 1:18-24 _Mary will give birth to Jesus_

2. Mark 6:3 _____

Why Do We Honor Mary?

We honor Mary because she was a real person who lived her life as best she could for God. That means that when she was a girl she probably ran and played and hollered like any normal child. As an adult she was concerned about what to fix for dinner or how to bandage the cut finger that Joseph got when he was working in the carpenter shop.

Mary also wondered about much more serious things like, "Why would God want me to be the Mother of Jesus?" She might even have thought that there must be someone who's better qualified or more experienced as a mother.

Mary lived her entire life in the best way possible. The Church says that Mary never committed a sin. She was tempted to do wrong and to be unkind, but she never did anything but the best and most correct thing. She was not an angel or a superhuman, just a human being doing the absolute best she could. She could have chosen to do something wrong, but she always chose to do what God wanted her to do.

Because God chose Mary for such an important job, she received special help. From the first moment of her existence on earth, Mary was especially favored and blessed by God. The Church describes this by saying that Mary was born without original sin. This special gift from God is called the Immaculate Conception of the Virgin Mary. It is celebrated with a special Mass on December 8. In the United States, it is a holy day of obligation — a day when all Catholics are expected to attend Mass.

Something to Do — God Wants You!

It's Saturday morning. You've just gotten comfortable on the couch to watch your favorite TV show. No one else is in the room but you. (If you always have brothers or sisters around when you're watching TV, pretend they're in the kitchen arguing over who gets the prize in the box of Sugar Frosted Fritos cereal.) Imagine that the TV screen loses its picture and glows pure white. You fiddle with the buttons and dials; you change channels, but nothing happens. The screen still glows white. Suddenly a voice comes from the set. It calls out *your* name! Then the voice says, "Don't be afraid. I'm bringing you a special message from God. God wants you to do something very important."

What is it that God wants you to do and what do you say to the voice? On your own piece of paper finish the rest of the story. There's no absolutely right or wrong answer. Just be honest and write down what you'd probably say and do.

If you're using this book in religion class or with your family, you could write a short play with different people taking turns being the TV voice and the viewer.

Praying With Mary

Catholics often talk about praying to Mary. It is important to remember, however, that when praying the rosary or other prayers involving Mary, we are praying *with* Mary *to* God. God is really the one to whom we pray. We do not actually pray *to* Mary (or the saints). Instead, we ask them to *intercede* for us. We ask them to help us pray to God and be our "go-between," our messenger between ourselves and God.

Prayer

Dear Mary,
     Whenever I'm afraid,
     angry, or alone,
     help me remember to ask you
     into my heart's home.
     You were the Mother of Jesus,
     with all its joy, sorrow, and pain.
     I know that you can hold me
     while I climb into his arms again.
     Amen.

5. What Child Is This?

Jesus Is the Long-awaited Savior

According to the Bible the Hebrew people had been waiting for nearly 2,000 years for the birth of the Savior. About 1,800 years before Jesus was born, Abraham learned about God and became known as the father of a great nation. His son Isaac and his grandchildren and great-grandchildren continued to believe that God had special plans for them.

Many years later, about 1,200 years before the birth of Christ, Moses became a great leader of this special group of people. In an event called the ''Exodus,'' he led them out of slavery in Egypt to a land that they could call their own where they would be free.

Two hundred years later, David became the king, the earthly ruler of God's Chosen People. He knew, however, that he was not the Messiah or Savior of the people. One who was much greater and more powerful would be born from his descendants — but not for another thousand years.

It is hard to imagine the hundreds and hundreds of years that people waited for the Messiah. It is easier to understand how long that wait lasted if we look at Jesus' family tree. In the first chapter of the Gospel of Matthew there is a long list of people's names. Most of the names are hard to pronounce! This list contains the names of many of Jesus' grandparents, great-grandparents, great-great-grandparents, and so on, all the way back to Abraham. If you said the word "great" at least thirty-eight times and then said "grandfather," that's who Abraham would be to Jesus. And that is counting only the people who are mentioned in the list. There are many other ancestors whose names were forgotten with the passage of time.

GREAT, GREAT, GREAT, GREAT, GREAT, GREAT, GREAT, GREAT, GREAT, GREAT, GREAT, GREAT, GREAT, GREAT, GREAT, GREAT, GREAT....

Jesus' Family Tree

A family tree is a chart or drawing listing your parents, brothers, sisters, grandparents, aunts, uncles, and other relatives. Sometimes a family will research their family tree to learn of their ancestors who lived hundreds of years ago. Some families will hang a chart of their family tree on a wall for everyone to see.

Jesus had a family tree, too. We trace it through his foster-father, Joseph. A verse in the Old Testament reads, "But a shoot shall sprout from the stump of Jesse, and from his roots a bud shall blossom" (Isaiah 11:1).

Jesse was one of Jesus' ancestors and the words in the passage talk about Jesus' family tree. The Gospel of Matthew, chapter 1, verses 1-17, gives a listing of many of Jesus' ancient relatives. In a sense, the entire Old Testament tells the story of Jesus' relatives. They were God's Chosen People, specially selected to bring the Good News of Salvation to the world through Jesus.

The Birth and Boyhood of Jesus

Only two of the four Gospels tell about the birth of Jesus. The first two chapters of the Gospel of Matthew and the first two chapters of the Gospel of Luke tell stories from the birth and early years of Jesus' life. The Gospels of Mark and John do not mention the birth of Jesus.

There are two reasons why the Gospel writers did not mention very much about the birth of Jesus. First, they probably did not know much about Jesus when he was growing up. Second, people didn't write things down, or if they did the information has been lost. Back in Jesus' time very few people knew how to read and write, and they had no cameras or tape recorders.

People simply told one another what was going on in their lives and their neighborhoods. Stories about Jesus' time on earth were told from one person to the next in much the same way that your grandparents or older neighbors and relatives tell you stories about the people they knew many years ago. Most of the stories that people remembered about Jesus had to do with what he did when he was a grown man.

Most of the stories about Jesus as a boy were forgotten because there was nothing really special about them. At the time Jesus was a child, very few people in his neighborhood suspected that he would grow up to be our Savior.

Something to Do —
Write Your Own Christmas Story

1. Read the first two chapters of both the Gospel of Matthew and the Gospel of Luke.
2. Go through the Christmas cards sent to you or your family. Pick out all the cards that picture parts of the Christmas story (angels, stable, shepherds, kings, etc.). Arrange these cards in the proper order from the start (Annunciation) to the finish (Three Kings) of the Christmas story as it is told in the Gospels.
3. If you cannot find a card for each part of the Christmas story, draw or write that part of the story on a small sheet of paper.
4. Check your story with the two Gospels and see how many details you remembered to include and how many you forgot.
5. Display your collection of cards for others to see during the Christmas season.

The Man
With 18 Names

When a new baby is about to come into the world, the baby's parents must decide what they will name their new child. Throughout the Bible, Jesus is known by many different names. Much of the time he is simply known as *Jesus,* but there are many places where he is called something different.

When you think about it, it's really not so unusual to have more than one name. Many people go by different names. For example, a woman may be known as "Mom" by her children, "Mrs. Voss" by the people who work for her, "Debbie" by her parents, and "Honey" by her husband. With all those names she's still the same person, but each name tells us something a little different about her.

The same thing is true for Jesus. Many Jews called him the *Messiah.* Messiah is the Hebrew word for "anointed one." The Messiah was the *Savior* the Jews were waiting for to come and save them from being destroyed. That Savior would be their King, the *King of the Jews.*

The Old Testament prophets called the coming Messiah, *Emmanuel.* That name means "God is with us." Jesus was God's Son here on earth with us. The name *Christ* was not Jesus' last name. It is a title that means the same thing as Messiah, except that Christ is a word in the Greek language while Messiah was a Hebrew word.

The apostles sometimes called Jesus *Rabbi,* the Hebrew word for teacher. When Jesus was called the *Nazorean* it was because that word told what town he was from — the town of Nazareth.

During Mass we say prayers that call Jesus the *Lamb of God*. When we call Jesus the Lamb of God, of course, we don't mean he was an animal. It means that he had the qualities of gentleness and meekness like a lamb. It also reminds us that during Jesus' time, a lamb was often the animal that people used as a sacrifice to God. People would kill a lamb and offer it to God as a sign of their love for God.

Sometimes people call Jesus the *Light of the World* because he brings bright rays of light and hope into our lives. Even when the world seems like a really crummy, dark, or scary place, Jesus is the Light who helps us see the right, bright path through life — the path that leads to faith, hope, and love for others and God.

Jesus is known by other names, too, which you can learn about as you grow up.

Something to Do —
The Many Names of Jesus

Here is a partial list of Jesus' names. They appear in all directions in the puzzle. Find them and circle them in the word finder puzzle.

CHRIST

EMMANUEL

IMMANUEL

JESUS

KING OF GLORY

KING OF THE JEWS

LAMB OF GOD

LIGHT OF THE WORLD

LORD

MESSIAH

NAZOREAN

PRINCE OF PEACE

RABBI

REDEEMER

SAVIOR

SON OF GOD

SON OF MAN

THE WORD

```
M O P S D H O W E A C G B N L D R O L U L
R U J A A O S W E J E H T F O G N I K H Z
L F I A R V A R J T E S F H T R H D M Z O
R I I E O I I S M S G O E E O S N E L I E
W R S L S E O O L O O F N L L O I V P T K
S N C E A Z D E R E T U W E R R F R F T I
U S D U I N I F C G S B U M A F I O H R N
N S O N O F M A N O O N J I B N H E M C G
T S Z A K R E R M A A L O E C G W O O G O
D Y G M M D M E P M E E N E S O I A N R F
A E E M N E K O M T E J O S R U E A I O G
D M H E O E C I O S N F L D O T S I F W L
O F M G R A H G M R P A P E O R Z A S D O
G C U I I R R R A E L N E A R A O L M E R
F I F I A O E F A N O M U R O E P G E E Y
O N S B I M N C E M S E M D O G F O N O S
B J B D E S E A M B O S A R N Z H G O D E
M I I E O F L S Z V N S T L O A A E L R H
A O D Y E O H E E O R I E H D A J N R T D
L E N D F E L W R C R A F M O N D G B B W
R K N S U D L R O W E H T F O T H G I L T
```

Prayer

Hi, Jesus. You sure had a lot of names! If I had that many names I wouldn't be able to keep track of them all. Now that I think about it, different people call me by different names, too. They are _____ and _____.
Sometimes I've been called names that are not nice, too. I get pretty mad or sad when that happens. I guess you know how that feels, too. People called you names when they were about to crucify you. I'm sorry for the times I've called people names and I want to try to do better. Please help me remember you whenever I'm tempted to call someone a bad name. Amen.

6. The Attack of the Killer Morzies

The True Meaning of Christmas

Have you ever found yourself feeling a little like the child in this picture? Have you ever received many nice gifts and still wanted more? If so, you've been bitten by a morzy. Morzies are those little (and sometimes not so little) thoughts inside you that are always wanting more of something. Morzies' favorite time of year is Christmas. They can also show up on birthdays, but during the Christmas season they multiply faster than mosquitoes in a swamp. No one is ever totally immune to morzy bites.

mor·zy / ˈmō(ə)rzē/ Any of numerous imaginary bugs that attack humans. This insect's bite causes a person to want *more* of many things, even if the person already has plenty. Morzy bites have also been known to keep people from sharing with one another.

Something to Do — The Morzy Quiz

Here's a quiz to help you figure out if you've ever been bitten by morzies. Answer yes or no to each question.

1. Does your hand ache after you've written down all the items on your Christmas wish list?
2. Are you more interested in what's inside a package than who gave it to you?
3. Have you ever been mad because you didn't get exactly what you wanted for Christmas?
4. On the day after Christmas do you find yourself already thinking of what you want next year?
5. Are you sad if you get "just clothes" as a Christmas present?
6. Have you ever felt jealous that someone else got more or nicer gifts than you did?
7. Have you ever found yourself not wanting to let a friend play with your presents?
8. Have you ever been angry with someone who bought you a cheap gift when you knew they could afford something better?
9. Do you forget to thank people for the gifts you receive?
10. On the day after Christmas have you ever gotten a sad feeling that makes you want to say, "Is that all there is to Christmas?"

Scoring:

If you answered "yes" to five or more of these questions, you have had a bad case of the morzies. If you said "yes" three to five times, you're about average. If you answered "yes" to two or less, you're probably not telling the truth. The truth is, *everyone* has been bitten by a morzy. Even parents, priests, the principal, your teacher, and the person who wrote this book have been bitten by a morzy at one time or another. Fortunately, there is more to Advent and Christmas than receiving expensive gifts. If you already know that, you are on the right track to understanding what Christmas and Christ's message are all about.

Jesus Tells Us About the Most Important Gift of All

One day Jesus told a group of people about the most important treasure in life. He said:

Do not store up for yourselves treasures on earth, where moth and decay destroy, and thieves break in and steal. But store up treasures in heaven, where neither moth nor decay destroys, nor thieves break in and steal. For where your treasure is, there also will your heart be (Matthew 6:19-21).

Jesus' words might puzzle you. His message will make more sense if you substitute the word *presents* for *treasures* and read the passage again. Basically, Jesus is telling us that we shouldn't make our earthly treasures (radios, games, bicycles, clothes, toys) the most important things in our lives. His words remind us that these things can break, wear out, and get stolen or lost. We can also get tired of them or outgrow them. You probably have old Christmas presents right now that you haven't played with or worn for a long time. Jesus wants us to store our "treasures" in heaven because what is in heaven lasts forever.

The kinds of things Jesus wants us to store up in heaven are things like helping Mom or Dad with household chores or cheering up your brother when he didn't make the basketball team or forgiving a friend for doing something you didn't like. Jesus tells us that following his ways should be the most important thing in our lives. It will guarantee that our reward in heaven will be great. On the other hand, if toys, games, tapes, books, money, a radio, and jewelry are most important to you — more important than people — then you will probably have a very sad life.

Some people have a lot of neat *things* but they are sad and lonely because they allow things to become more important than people. People are always more important than things.

When he talked about storing up treasures in heaven, Jesus was also telling us something about Christmas and gift giving. He told us that the best gift we can give to Jesus and to others for Christmas is the gift of ourselves.

Something to Do —
A New Kind of Christmas Gift

Buying Christmas gifts can be expensive, especially when you're a kid. One of the best gifts you can give someone is the gift of yourself. How do you give yourself for Christmas? It's easier than you think.

Get some fancy colored paper, some marking pens, and crayons. Make up coupons that list what you promise to do for someone. For example, you could make up coupons that say, ''I will make your bed for one full week'' and give a few of those coupons to your brother. Then, when he would like you to make his bed for a week he gives you one of the coupons and you would make his bed for a week.

Make coupons for many different things that you can do for others: an afternoon of raking leaves or mowing the lawn, helping with grocery shopping, setting the table, taking out trash, cleaning the bathroom, washing the car, washing dishes or loading the dishwasher, clearing off the table, walking the dog, vacuuming, dusting, giving backrubs. The list is endless.

Put the coupon in a fancy envelope and put a bow on it so that it looks like a special certificate. Just remember that if you decide to give these coupon gifts, you really have to do what the coupon promises, or else your gift won't really be much of a gift.

Jesus Never Forgot the Poor

During Advent we see all kinds of commercials on TV and hear ads on the radio for Christmas presents. When you go to the store there are Christmas decorations everywhere to give you the holiday feeling and to get you and your family to BUY, BUY, BUY until your wallets are empty.

There is nothing wrong with spending money and buying gifts. Jesus is not a Scrooge who hates Christmas and happy people. He likes people to be happy and to give and receive gifts at Christmas. After all, Christmas is a special time for Jesus because it celebrates his birth at Bethlehem.

While we remember Jesus' birth we should also remember his life and his words. Many of Jesus' words and actions were intended to help the poor, the sick, and the needy. He saw many rich people neglecting the poor. He saw sick people getting no help for their illnesses. He felt sad because people with disabilities had such difficulties in living their daily lives.

Jesus reminded the people to help their less fortunate sisters and brothers and neighbors. Christmas is a special time to help these people in need but it is more important to help the poor all year long. Many local newspapers and radio stations collect money for the needy. Some churches and organizations like the Boy Scouts and the Girl Scouts gather food and clothing for the poor and the elderly. What can you do to help people who are in need?

Prayer

Dear Jesus, Christmas can get so complicated! I get excited about getting presents and worry about giving them. Sometimes I get angry about the chores I have to do at Christmas time or the goofy way my family wants to decorate the tree. Through all of this, Jesus, help me remember the true meaning of Christmas. It is for remembering you and how you want us to give love to you by giving love to others. Help me to show my love by giving gifts and giving myself in service to others. Amen.

7. The Christmas That Never Ends

Jesus Is With Us Always

'Twas the day after Christmas
and all through the mall
people were returning gifts
that were too big or too small.

The lines were all long.
Small children were cranky.
One boy cried, "I didn't get what I wanted!"
His dad grumbled, "It cost too much, Frankie."

Does this sound anything like a day after Christmas that *you've* had? If not, that's good; but if you've had a bad day or felt sad right after Christmas you're pretty normal. Lots of people (even adults) feel sort of "down in the dumps" right after Christmas. That's because preparing for Christmas takes a month or two, but then when Christmas finally comes it's over in just one short day!

Before Christmas most radio stations play Christmas music, the stores have special decorations and lights, and there are special programs on TV. On the day after Christmas that all stops very suddenly. If you visit most stores (and even some people's homes) a day or two after Christmas you'll notice they're already taking down the decorations and turning off the special lights. The Christmas trees are already put away in a box, sitting outside with the trash, or burning in the fireplace. No wonder many people get sad after Christmas!

Even the statue of Baby Jesus gets wrapped up in tissue paper and put away in some box, too. You know, of course, that Jesus didn't (and shouldn't) just disappear. Jesus should live in our hearts forever. As young Christians we can keep the spirit of Christmas alive long after they stop playing Jingle Bells on the radio.

Christmas Time Is Family Time

The Sunday after Christmas is usually known as Holy Family Sunday. At Mass the lector will read from the Bible about how we can have the happy kind of family that God wants us all to have. The priest will read a story from the

Gospel about Jesus, Mary, and Joseph as an example for our families.

While Jesus was growing up he didn't have a lot of the things we now have to occupy our time. He didn't watch television. There was no radio to listen to, nor were there movies to rent or video games to play. Football hadn't even been invented yet. The Holy Family probably spent their spare time talking about their day, praying, playing games, and telling the traditional stories about God's people.

Something to Do —
A Family New Year's Resolution

Right after Christmas people are usually thinking about the coming new year. This is the time when people make New Year's resolutions. They decide to give up something bad or do something good that will help them be a better person in the coming year. Some people go on a diet, others try to stop smoking. Even kids can make resolutions like getting to bed on time or finishing homework before dinner each day.

Your whole family can resolve to have *Family Night* once a week in the coming year. Family Night should be a night with no television (it's not as rough as it sounds), no outside company, and no plans to go somewhere else. If you can, unplug the telephone or turn on the answering machine. On this night the family could make popcorn and cocoa, and then take turns reading out loud from the Bible or another good book. You could read a play together with each person taking a different part. You could also play cards or some other game, or, better still, make something together (like assembling a jigsaw puzzle). Whatever you do should be good for the whole family.

During the Christmas season have your first Family Night. Decide what you want to do on future Family Nights. You can also decide what will be the best night of the week. On a large sheet of paper write the rules that your family will follow for Family Nights. Make this a fancy sign and allow space for all family members to sign the paper. It will be their pledge to keep this family resolution. Then hang this paper where all can see and remember their family resolution for the New Year.

What Happened to Jesus After Christmas?

The Bible tells us several stories of events that happened right after Jesus' birth. The Church also helps us remember important events and people in Jesus' life with special days right after Christmas.

Chapter 2 of the Gospel of Matthew tells the happy story of the Wise Men coming to see Jesus and the very sad story of the wicked King Herod killing the young infants. It also explains how Joseph led Jesus and Mary to safety in Egypt.

Chapter 2, verses 21 to 52, of the Gospel of Luke is filled with stories about Jesus being taken to the temple as a little baby and his parents speaking with Simeon and Anna. We also learn about Jesus getting lost in the temple during a family trip to the holy city of Jerusalem.

Follow That Star!

Have you ever watched old detective or cops and robbers shows? Someone always seems to jump in a car and holler at the driver, "Follow that car!" Well, in a way that might be what the three Wise Men (also known as the Three Kings or the Magi) did long ago. Only they said, "Follow that *star*!" instead of "Follow that car." The star they followed is the one that led them to Jesus.

Think about what a star can mean. A star can be someone who's famous in the movies. It can be the mark you get on a good paper in school. Generals in the army often wear a star or stars on their uniforms to show their power and importance. Fireworks can also look like stars. When you really

think about it, a star nearly always is trying to tell us, "Hey! Look here! Here's something really important!"

Stars are also, of course, those tiny lights in the night sky. They tell us that there is something out there, something that is not of this world. When people look up at the stars they often start wondering, "What's out there?" or even "*Who* is out there?"

The Star That Leads to Jesus

Advent has been a time for us to travel through time and space toward Jesus. Remember the three Wise Men who brought gifts to Baby Jesus? These men traveled from very far away to bring their gifts of gold, frankincense, and myrrh. Back in those days the Wise Men couldn't just jump in their car and take the highway straight to Bethlehem. On foot and probably on camels they had to travel many, many miles to find the Child who was King of the Jews. They didn't know exactly where to find Jesus and there weren't any signs showing them the way, either.

Long ago people used the stars to help them find their way when they were traveling. The Wise Men are called "wise" because they were experts on the stars. They knew that a new star had appeared in the sky and that it was a sign from God that a king had been born. So they followed that star!

Something to Do —
How Wise Are You About the Wise Men?

If you read the story about the Wise Men in the Bible, you should be able to complete this crossword puzzle. For help, read Matthew 2:1-12.

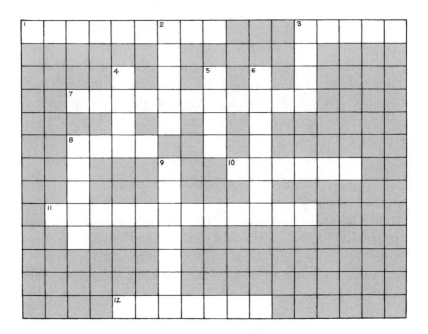

ACROSS

1. Town where Jesus was born.
3. Name of the newborn King.
7. Occupation of the Wise Men.
8. Mother of Jesus.
10. The Wise Men visited Jesus so they could do him _____ .
11. One of the gifts from the Wise Men.
12. Jesus was the _____ .

DOWN

2. Jesus was born during this king's reign.
3. The people of Israel.
4. What led the Wise Men to Jesus?
5. Another gift.
6. Baby Jesus was the _____ king.
8. Third gift of the Wise Men.
9. Herod summoned the chief _____ .

Following the Star Today and Always

Following a star over a long trip was probably frustrating for the people in Jesus' day. First, it meant that they had to do much of their traveling at night. Second, what if it was cloudy or rainy? How could they see the stars then? The Wise Men continued their long journey because they had faith in God's plan for them. They could not *see* Jesus nor did they even know that he was in Bethlehem. They were not sure exactly what was going to happen. All they could do was prepare as best they could and trust God with everything else.

Your life and everyone else's life is a little bit like that. We never really know what is going to happen to us or when. Yes, we can predict things like tomorrow's scout meeting or next week's science test. Even those things can change, though, if the scoutmaster gets sick or the science test is put off a day so the teacher can cover more material.

Because life can be so unpredictable, Jesus said, "Be

watchful! Be alert! You do not know when the time will come'' (Mark 13:33). When Jesus said this he was talking about the coming of the end of the world. Now the end of the world sounds scary to many people because they can't predict what will happen or when the end will come. They also worry about what will happen to them.

If you follow the star, walk in the light of Christ, and observe the teachings of Jesus, you have nothing to fear. If you prepare for the coming of the Lord at Christmas each year, if you live in love and help people in need, if you pray and welcome Christ into your heart each day, you will be prepared for the final coming of Christ. Whether Christ calls you back to himself when you are still young or whether you live a long life on earth, you can be assured that the Lord will welcome you into your heavenly home if you have prepared for his coming each Advent season and each day of the year.

Prayer

Dear God, the Wise Men were pretty brave, if you ask me. They traveled all that distance with only a star to show them the way to Jesus. That shows a deep trust and faith in you. If it had been me, I probably would have been worrying about what I'd eat, if I was going in the totally wrong direction, and whether there were any rest stops. Whenever I feel lost or mixed up or confused or worried, help me remember the Wise Men who simply put things in your hands. Then they kept going. Sure enough, they finally got to exactly the right place at the right time. Thank you for helping me on my trip through life every day. Help me to prepare each day for your Final Coming in my life. Amen.

Did you like this book? Do you have any ideas for how it could be different or better? Do you need answers to any of the games or puzzles? If you do, write to:

Julie Kelemen
Liguori Publications
One Liguori Drive
Liguori, MO 63057